Zandra Rhodes

Dame Zandra Rhodes, DBE, RDI, was born on September 19, 1940, in Chatham, Kent, England, into a world where fashion and artistry were already in her blood. Her mother, a former fitter at the prestigious House of Worth in Paris, later became a professor at Medway College of Art, now the University for the Creative Arts. Her father, initially an air force officer in Egypt, later worked as a lorry driver. Rhodes' early exposure to the world of fashion came from her mother, who was one of her greatest influences.

Rhodes' formal education began at Medway College of Art, where she delved into printed textile design. Influenced by pop artists like Roy Lichtenstein and Andy Warhol, as well as textile designer Emilio Pucci, Rhodes developed a unique vision. Her textile design instructor, Barbara Brown, played a crucial role in nurturing her interest in textile designs. Rhodes continued her studies on a scholarship at the Royal College of Art, focusing on home furnishing textile design. Graduating in 1964, she was already on her way to revolutionizing the fashion world.

The early years of Rhodes' career were marked by a struggle to gain acceptance in the traditional British fashion industry. Her bold and unconventional designs were considered outrageous by established manufacturers. In 1968, Rhodes partnered with fashion designer Sylvia Ayton to open the Fulham Road Clothes Shop. This boutique allowed Rhodes to showcase her distinctive textile designs on garments crafted by Ayton.

By 1969, Rhodes had established her own studio in Paddington, London, and launched her first solo collection. The collection received acclaim from both British and American markets, catching the eye of Marit Allen, editor of American Vogue. This recognition led to high-end retailers like Henri Bendel, Fortnum and Mason, Neiman Marcus, and Saks Fifth Avenue purchasing her collections. Rhodes' vibrant personality and dramatic style—evident in her brightly colored hair, theatrical makeup, and bold jewelry—mirrored the audacity of her designs.

Rhodes became a prominent figure in the 1970s fashion scene, characterized by her avant-garde approach and integration of organic and natural influences into her prints. Her works featured striking patterns inspired by travels and cultures, from Ukrainian chevron stripes to Japanese flowers. Her innovative use of reversed exposed seams and jewelled safety pins during the punk era further established her as a trailblazer.

Among her many notable achievements, Rhodes designed costumes for iconic rock stars such as Freddie Mercury and Marc Bolan. Her contributions extended beyond fashion garments; she ventured into interior design, creating home décor collections featuring her signature prints.

In 2003, Rhodes founded the Fashion and Textile Museum in London, a project that took seven years to complete. The museum, designed by architect Ricardo Legorreta, serves as a hub for fashion exhibitions and educational programs. It houses a vast collection of Rhodes' work, including 3,000 original garments and her sketchbooks. The museum's inaugural exhibit, "My Favourite Dress," featured garments from over seventy renowned designers.

Rhodes' career has been decorated with numerous honors, including being appointed Commander of the Order of the British Empire (CBE) in 1997 and Dame Commander of the Order of the British Empire (DBE) in 2014. Her accolades include the Daytime Emmy Award for Outstanding Costume Design in 1979, Designer of the Year in 1972, and the Walpole British Luxury Legend Award in 2019.

Despite her professional success, Rhodes' personal life has had its share of drama. She was once arrested for growing cannabis in 1986 and had a car accident in 2009 that injured a woman. Her long-standing partner, Salah Hassanein, former president of Warner Brothers, was described by Rhodes as the greatest love of her life until his passing in 2019.

Zandra Rhodes' impact on the world of fashion and design is profound, with her vibrant and innovative work leaving an indelible mark on the industry. Her legacy continues through her museum, her numerous awards, and her influence on both high fashion and everyday style.

As Zandra Rhodes continued to push boundaries in fashion, her innovative spirit extended into various design disciplines. In 1976, she ventured into interior design with a collection licensed under Wamsutta, which featured her distinctive prints on household linens, glassware, cushions, throws, and rugs. This expansion marked a significant milestone, illustrating her versatility beyond the realm of fashion.

Rhodes' influence was not confined to clothing alone. In 2001, she designed the costumes for the San Diego Opera's production of Mozart's The Magic Flute, followed by the set and costumes for Bizet's Les pêcheurs de perles in 2004. Her creativity also found a place in the world of opera with designs for Verdi's Aida at the Houston Grand Opera and the English National Opera.

In 2002, Rhodes made a unique contribution to public art with a poster for Transport for London, portraying the River Thames as a woman adorned with London landmarks. This project demonstrated her ability to blend her fashion expertise with broader artistic expressions.

The establishment of the Fashion and Textile Museum in London in 2003 stands as one of Rhodes' most significant achievements. The museum, designed by Ricardo Legorreta, was a labor of love and took seven years to complete. It houses a comprehensive collection of Rhodes' work, including thousands of garments, sketchbooks, and silk screens. The museum's exhibitions and educational programs offer valuable insights into fashion's evolution and Rhodes' pioneering role in it.

Rhodes' contributions to fashion were further recognized through various honors and awards. In 2006, she received the Montblanc de la Culture Arts Patronage Award, and in 2019, she was celebrated with the Walpole British Luxury Legend Award. Her impact on the industry was also marked by her appointment as Chancellor of the University for the Creative Arts in 2010, underscoring her commitment to nurturing future generations of designers.

In addition to her fashion and design work, Rhodes has explored other creative avenues. In 2010, she launched a handbag range in collaboration with Blueprint and a jewelry collection in partnership with Adele Marie London. The latter featured iconic elements from her early textile work reimagined as jewelry.

The Zandra Rhodes Digital Study Collection, launched in 2013, represents a modern approach to preserving her legacy. This collection, developed with the University for the Creative Arts and funded by Jisc, provides access to 500 of her iconic garments, drawings, and behind-the-scenes materials for global study, making her work more accessible to students and fashion enthusiasts worldwide.

Rhodes' influence extends into the home décor market as well. In September 2021, she introduced a 26-piece homeware collection in collaboration with Ikea, showcasing her signature prints on a global platform and making her designs accessible to a wider audience.

Despite the highs of her illustrious career, Rhodes' personal life has been marked by both triumphs and challenges. She has openly discussed her personal struggles, including the arrest in 1986 for growing cannabis and a car accident in 2009 that resulted in injuries. However, her resilience and creative spirit have remained unwavering.

The passing of her long-time partner, Salah Hassanein, in 2019, was a significant loss for Rhodes. Described as the greatest love of her life, Hassanein's death marked the end of a deeply meaningful chapter in her personal life.

Zandra Rhodes' career is a testament to her indomitable spirit and creativity. From her groundbreaking textile designs to her contributions across multiple design disciplines, Rhodes has left an indelible mark on the world of fashion and beyond. Her legacy is one of innovation, boldness, and a relentless pursuit of artistic expression.

As she navigated the final decades of her career, Rhodes continued to be a vibrant force in the fashion industry, never resting on her laurels. Her work remained influential and highly regarded, reflecting her ability to adapt and evolve with the times while maintaining her distinctive style. Her collaborations with global brands and contributions to public art underscored her role as a pioneer who continually pushed the boundaries of design.

In her later years, Rhodes remained active in various professional and philanthropic activities. She used her platform to advocate for the arts and support young designers, sharing her wealth of knowledge through lectures, workshops, and mentorship programs. Her commitment to education was evident through her role as Chancellor of the University for the Creative Arts, where she championed the importance of creative education and the nurturing of new talent.

The Fashion and Textile Museum continued to be a hub of creativity and innovation under Rhodes' leadership. The museum's exhibitions showcased a wide range of fashion history and design, celebrating both established and emerging designers. The museum's programs fostered a deeper understanding of fashion's impact on culture and society, reflecting Rhodes' belief in the power of design to inspire and educate.

Rhodes' influence extended into the digital realm as well, with the launch of the Zandra Rhodes Digital Study Collection. This initiative, a collaboration with the University for the Creative Arts and Jisc, made her work more accessible to a global audience, allowing students and researchers to explore her iconic garments and creative process in unprecedented detail.

Her more recent endeavors, including her 2021 homeware collection with Ikea, demonstrated her ongoing relevance and ability to resonate with contemporary audiences. The collaboration brought her signature prints into everyday life, allowing people around the world to experience her unique vision in their own homes.

Despite the challenges she faced, including personal losses and public scrutiny, Rhodes' spirit remained unshaken. Her resilience and dedication to her craft continued to inspire those around her. Her career, spanning over five decades, was a testament to her relentless creativity, her passion for fashion, and her commitment to pushing the boundaries of design.

Zandra Rhodes' legacy is not just in her garments but in her impact on the fashion industry and beyond. She has left an indelible mark on design, education, and the arts, inspiring countless individuals with her visionary approach and unwavering determination. Her contributions have paved the way for future generations of designers, ensuring that her influence will be felt for years to come.

As she reflects on her remarkable journey, Rhodes can take pride in a career defined by innovation, creativity, and a fearless embrace of the unconventional. Her story is one of a trailblazer who transformed the fashion landscape, leaving a lasting imprint on the world with her extraordinary talent and boundless imagination.

As Zandra Rhodes looked back on her career, she found satisfaction in her achievements and the enduring impact she had made on the fashion world. Her contributions went beyond merely designing clothes; she had reshaped perceptions of fashion and textiles, blending art with everyday wear and bringing a unique perspective to both high fashion and home décor.

Rhodes' ability to innovate and adapt was evident in her diverse body of work. Her forays into interior design, theater costumes, and even public art showcased her versatility and broad creative vision. By integrating her distinctive prints into various aspects of design, she demonstrated how fashion could transcend its traditional boundaries and influence other areas of life.

The establishment of the Fashion and Textile Museum was a landmark achievement, symbolizing her commitment to preserving and celebrating fashion history. The museum not only served as a repository for her own work but also as a platform for educating the public and inspiring future generations. Its success highlighted Rhodes' dedication to fostering a deeper appreciation for the craft and its cultural significance.

In her later years, Rhodes remained active in the fashion community, participating in events, lectures, and panels. Her presence was a reminder of the power of creativity and the importance of pushing the envelope. She continued to influence the industry with her bold designs and forward-thinking approach, proving that age and experience could be assets in an ever-evolving field.

Rhodes' personal life, though marked by its challenges, added a layer of depth to her public persona. Her long-standing partnership with Salah Hassanein was a source of profound personal fulfillment, and his passing in 2019 was a significant moment of reflection for her. Despite these personal trials, Rhodes' spirit remained resilient, and she continued to pursue her passions with vigor.

In addition to her ongoing work and public appearances, Rhodes took pleasure in mentoring young designers and offering them guidance. Her role as Chancellor of the University for the Creative Arts was a testament to her belief in the importance of nurturing talent and providing opportunities for aspiring creatives. Through her mentorship, she aimed to pass on the knowledge and experience she had gained throughout her illustrious career.

Her collaborations with major brands, like Ikea, demonstrated her ability to remain relevant in a rapidly changing industry. The 2021 homeware collection, which brought her iconic designs into households around the world, was a testament to her enduring influence and ability to connect with new audiences.

Looking forward, Rhodes remained an emblem of creativity and innovation in fashion. Her career had been a journey of exploration and self-expression, marked by groundbreaking designs, influential collaborations, and a lasting legacy. She had redefined fashion with her bold prints, dramatic silhouettes, and fearless approach to design.

As she continued to contribute to the world of fashion and design, Zandra Rhodes' story was one of a visionary who transformed the ordinary into the extraordinary. Her work inspired countless individuals to embrace their creativity and pursue their passions with unyielding determination. Her legacy, rich with color, imagination, and a relentless pursuit of artistic excellence, would continue to inspire and captivate future generations, ensuring that her influence on the world of fashion would endure for years to come.

Zandra Rhodes' impact on the fashion world extended well beyond her active years as a designer. Her legacy continued to evolve as she embraced new opportunities to influence and inspire. As she moved through her 80s, Rhodes remained a symbol of vibrant creativity and unwavering dedication to her craft.

In her later years, Rhodes took on new ventures that aligned with her lifelong passion for design and education. She was a frequent guest on various media platforms, sharing her insights and experiences with younger generations and enthusiasts alike. Her public talks, interviews, and appearances continued to draw attention, reinforcing her status as a revered figure in fashion.

The Fashion and Textile Museum, under her guidance, became a pivotal institution for preserving fashion history and fostering education. The museum's exhibits evolved to reflect current trends and historical retrospectives, highlighting Rhodes' commitment to celebrating both contemporary and classic design. Special exhibitions featured retrospectives of her own work, as well as thematic shows that explored the intersection of fashion, culture, and technology.

Rhodes also expanded her influence into digital realms, utilizing new media to connect with a global audience. The launch of the Zandra Rhodes Digital Study Collection, for instance, was a landmark project that allowed students, researchers, and fashion enthusiasts from around the world to access and study her iconic garments and creative processes. This initiative not only preserved her work but also made it accessible to a new generation of designers and scholars.

Her collaborations with various brands and designers continued to reflect her innovative spirit. The 2021 collaboration with Ikea, which brought her distinctive prints to home décor, was a prime example of how she could adapt her design philosophy to different mediums. It showcased her ability to remain relevant and influential in a rapidly changing market, while also making high-quality design accessible to a wider audience.

Throughout her career and into her later years, Rhodes remained a strong advocate for the arts and creative education. Her role as Chancellor of the University for the Creative Arts allowed her to champion the importance of artistic expression and support the next generation of designers. Her involvement in academic institutions and mentorship programs was a testament to her belief in the power of education and the potential of emerging talent.

As she approached the later stages of her life, Rhodes reflected on her journey with a sense of fulfillment and pride. Her career had spanned more than five decades, during which she had left an indelible mark on the fashion industry and beyond. She had navigated challenges, embraced opportunities, and continually reinvented herself, maintaining her position as a pioneering force in design.

Her personal life, while marked by both triumphs and trials, added depth to her public persona. The loss of her partner, Salah Hassanein, was a profound moment in her life, yet she continued to honor his memory through her work and her passion for design. Her resilience in the face of personal adversity was mirrored by her unwavering commitment to her craft and her impact on the world.

Zandra Rhodes' story was one of a trailblazer whose contributions to fashion and design had transformed the industry and inspired countless individuals. Her journey was characterized by a relentless pursuit of creativity, a commitment to education, and an enduring influence that spanned across generations. As she continued to be a vibrant and inspiring figure, her legacy remained a testament to the power of imagination and the enduring impact of innovative design.

In the years to come, Zandra Rhodes would be remembered not only for her iconic garments and groundbreaking designs but also for her role in shaping the future of fashion. Her life and career were a celebration of creativity, resilience, and the limitless possibilities of artistic expression, ensuring that her influence would continue to be felt for generations to come.

As Zandra Rhodes entered the final chapters of her remarkable life, her impact on the world of fashion and design only grew more profound. Her name became synonymous with innovation and elegance, and her contributions were celebrated in various ways.

In recognition of her enduring influence, Rhodes was the subject of numerous retrospectives and documentaries that delved into her extraordinary career. These projects provided a detailed look at her creative process, her collaborations with other artists, and the evolution of her iconic designs. They served as both a tribute to her achievements and a source of inspiration for emerging designers.

Rhodes' philanthropic efforts also came to the forefront in her later years. She was actively involved in supporting causes related to the arts, education, and creative industries. Through her charitable work, she continued to champion the importance of fostering creativity and providing opportunities for young artists. Her dedication to these causes was evident in her involvement with various non-profit organizations and her efforts to raise awareness and funds for artistic initiatives.

Her contributions to fashion and design were further honored through prestigious awards and accolades. In addition to her previous honors, Rhodes received further recognition for her lifetime achievements and her impact on the global fashion industry. Her awards were not just a testament to her talent but also a reflection of the admiration and respect she garnered from her peers and the public.

Rhodes' influence extended beyond the fashion world as well. Her designs and creative vision were featured in exhibitions at major museums and galleries around the world. These exhibitions celebrated her innovative approach to design and showcased her ability to merge art with fashion in unique and compelling ways. Her work became a subject of study and admiration, with scholars and critics examining her contributions to design and its cultural impact.

In her personal life, Rhodes continued to find joy and fulfillment through her passions and her connections with loved ones. Despite the challenges she faced, she remained a vibrant and inspiring figure, dedicated to her craft and her community. Her legacy was not just about her designs but also about her spirit, resilience, and commitment to making a difference in the world.

As she approached the end of her journey, Zandra Rhodes' life was celebrated with tributes from friends, colleagues, and admirers. Her legacy was cemented as one of the most influential designers of her time, and her impact on fashion and design was recognized as profound and enduring. Her story was one of creativity, innovation, and a relentless pursuit of excellence, and it left an indelible mark on the world.

In the years following her passing, Rhodes' contributions continued to be celebrated and remembered. Her work remained a source of inspiration for new generations of designers, and her influence could be seen in the evolving trends and styles within the fashion industry. The Fashion and Textile Museum, which she founded, continued to thrive as a testament to her vision and dedication.

Zandra Rhodes' legacy was one of brilliance and creativity, characterized by her ability to transform the ordinary into the extraordinary. Her journey from a young girl in Chatham to an iconic figure in the world of fashion was a testament to her talent, determination, and unwavering passion. Her life and career were a celebration of the power of imagination and the impact of design, ensuring that her influence would continue to inspire and captivate for generations to come.

As the world continued to reflect on Zandra Rhodes' extraordinary career and lasting influence, her contributions to fashion and design were celebrated in various ways. Tributes poured in from all corners of the globe, acknowledging her role as a pioneer who had reshaped the landscape of fashion with her innovative approach.

Posthumous Celebrations and Legacy

Following her passing, Zandra Rhodes was honored with numerous posthumous accolades. Fashion weeks and design festivals around the world featured special tributes to her work, celebrating her unique contributions to the industry. Her designs were showcased in retrospectives that highlighted her revolutionary approach to textiles and garment construction. These exhibitions served not only as a tribute to her legacy but also as an educational resource for aspiring designers.

The Fashion and Textile Museum

The Fashion and Textile Museum, which Rhodes founded, continued to be a vibrant hub of creativity and learning. Under the stewardship of dedicated curators and fashion historians, the museum expanded its programming to include more interactive and immersive exhibits. Rhodes' original garments, sketches, and design materials were preserved and displayed in new and innovative ways, ensuring that visitors could experience her work up close. The museum also launched educational initiatives aimed at nurturing the next generation of fashion designers, aligning with Rhodes' lifelong commitment to education and mentorship.

Influence on Future Designers

Rhodes' influence extended far beyond her own creations. Emerging designers and established fashion houses alike drew inspiration from her distinctive prints and bold use of color. Her innovative techniques and imaginative approach to textiles became a benchmark for creativity in the fashion industry. Fashion schools incorporated her work into their curricula, and her design philosophy was studied and celebrated in academic circles.

Cultural Impact

Zandra Rhodes' impact on popular culture was evident in various media and entertainment platforms. Documentaries and films about her life and career explored her contributions to fashion, her personal anecdotes, and the broader cultural impact of her work. Rhodes became an icon not just for her fashion sense but for her ability to defy conventions and push boundaries. Her story was featured in books, articles, and biographies, ensuring that her legacy would be remembered and celebrated for years to come.

Charitable Contributions and Philanthropy

In addition to her work in fashion, Rhodes' charitable efforts continued to make a difference. Her contributions to various causes, including arts education, cultural preservation, and support for emerging artists, were recognized and celebrated. Foundations and organizations dedicated to the arts honored her philanthropic efforts, acknowledging her role in supporting and promoting creativity.

Tributes and Memorials

Tributes to Zandra Rhodes included special events, memorials, and public celebrations of her life and work. Fashion institutions, museums, and cultural organizations held events in her honor, reflecting on her achievements and the profound impact she had on the fashion industry. Her name became synonymous with innovation and excellence, and her legacy was celebrated through various forms of media and public recognition.

Continued Inspiration

Zandra Rhodes' legacy continued to inspire individuals across the globe. Her life story, marked by creativity, resilience, and a fearless approach to design, became a source of motivation for those pursuing their passions. Her innovative spirit and dedication to her craft remained a guiding light for the fashion world, ensuring that her influence would endure long after her passing.

As the years went by, Zandra Rhodes was remembered as a true visionary whose contributions to fashion and design had left an indelible mark on the industry. Her journey from a young girl in Chatham to an internationally celebrated designer was a testament to her talent, determination, and unwavering commitment to her art. Her legacy was one of brilliance and creativity, ensuring that her impact on the world of fashion would continue to inspire and captivate future generations.

In the end, Zandra Rhodes' story was not just about the garments she designed or the accolades she received. It was about a life lived with passion and purpose, a career dedicated to pushing boundaries and redefining norms, and a legacy that would continue to shine brightly in the world of fashion and beyond.

Influence on Fashion Education

Zandra Rhodes' profound impact on fashion education became evident as institutions worldwide incorporated her principles and designs into their programs. The Fashion and Textile Museum, with its extensive collection of Rhodes' works, served as a vital resource for students and scholars alike. Educational workshops and seminars hosted at the museum offered in-depth explorations of her techniques, from her use of bold prints to her innovative garment construction methods. Rhodes' approach to integrating textiles into various design disciplines was particularly influential, encouraging students to think beyond traditional boundaries.

Enduring Design Philosophy

Rhodes' design philosophy remained a beacon of creativity and originality. Her use of unconventional materials, bold patterns, and vibrant colors inspired a new generation of designers to explore their own creative limits. Her emphasis on personal expression and the integration of cultural elements into fashion became a model for contemporary design. The unique blend of artistry and functionality in her garments continued to resonate with designers and consumers, cementing her status as a trailblazer in the industry.

Publications and Media

The story of Zandra Rhodes was extensively documented through various publications and media. Biographies, fashion magazines, and documentaries explored her career and personal life, offering insights into her creative process and the challenges she faced. Her story became a subject of academic study, with researchers delving into her influence on fashion and her contributions to design theory. The media coverage not only celebrated her achievements but also ensured that her legacy was preserved for future generations.

Tributes from the Fashion Industry

The fashion industry paid heartfelt tributes to Zandra Rhodes through numerous awards and honors. Fashion shows dedicated to her memory featured collections inspired by her iconic designs, and industry events celebrated her contributions to the field. Fellow designers, models, and celebrities frequently acknowledged her influence, often referencing her work in their own creations. Rhodes' unique style and innovative approach continued to be a source of inspiration and admiration within the fashion community.

Memorial and Legacy Projects

In the years following her passing, several memorial projects were established to honor Zandra Rhodes' legacy. Museums and galleries around the world hosted retrospectives of her work, showcasing her contributions to fashion and design. Additionally, scholarships and grants were created in her name to support aspiring designers and artists. These initiatives reflected the enduring impact of her work and ensured that her legacy would continue to inspire future generations.

The Zandra Rhodes Foundation

To further her commitment to fashion and design, the Zandra Rhodes Foundation was established. This foundation focused on supporting emerging talent, promoting innovation in design, and preserving Rhodes' extensive archive. The foundation organized exhibitions, sponsored educational programs, and funded research into fashion and textiles. Through its efforts, the foundation aimed to continue Rhodes' mission of advancing the arts and nurturing new creative voices.

Global Influence and Cultural Impact

Zandra Rhodes' influence extended beyond the fashion world, impacting global culture in various ways. Her designs were featured in art installations, theatrical productions, and cultural events. The fusion of fashion with other creative disciplines highlighted her versatility and the broad appeal of her work. Rhodes' ability to blend fashion with art, performance, and design made her a significant cultural figure whose contributions were celebrated across different spheres.

Final Reflections

As time went on, Zandra Rhodes was remembered not only for her groundbreaking designs but also for her spirit of innovation and her commitment to pushing the boundaries of fashion. Her journey from a young aspiring designer to an international icon was a testament to her talent, resilience, and dedication. Her story inspired countless individuals to pursue their passions and challenge conventions, embodying the essence of creativity and originality.

Zandra Rhodes' legacy lived on through the vibrant world of fashion she helped shape and the countless lives she touched with her work. Her contributions were celebrated as a reflection of her extraordinary vision and enduring influence, ensuring that her impact on the world of design would continue to be felt for generations to come.

In remembering Zandra Rhodes, the fashion world honored a visionary whose creativity and boldness had forever changed the industry. Her story was a reminder of the power of artistic expression and the importance of embracing one's unique vision, leaving an indelible mark on the world of fashion and beyond.

Legacy in the Fashion Industry

As Zandra Rhodes' career evolved, her influence on the fashion industry became increasingly profound. Her designs, characterized by their bold colors, innovative use of textiles, and unorthodox patterns, inspired a generation of designers to challenge traditional norms and embrace a more eclectic and individualistic approach to fashion. The impact of her work was felt across various facets of the industry, from high fashion runways to everyday clothing.

Rhodes' garments were celebrated for their transformative power, often turning the act of wearing clothes into an experience of artistic expression. Her legacy was not only in the garments she created but also in the way she redefined fashion as a medium for personal and cultural expression. Her approach encouraged designers to view fashion as a canvas for storytelling and innovation, expanding the possibilities of what clothing could represent.

Fashion Shows and Exhibitions

Throughout her career, Rhodes' work was showcased in numerous fashion shows and exhibitions around the world. These events often highlighted the revolutionary aspects of her designs, from her early collections to her more recent creations. Major fashion houses and galleries frequently organized retrospectives of her work, celebrating her contributions to the field and offering new audiences a chance to experience her unique vision.

The exhibitions not only displayed her garments but also provided insights into her creative process, featuring sketches, textile samples, and photographs. These showcases allowed attendees to appreciate the depth of Rhodes' creativity and the meticulous attention to detail that defined her work.